"In his life-changing book, *Fields of the Fatherless*, Tom Davis shines a bright light on the true meaning of living out the gospel. His much-needed message reminds us of the urgency and frequency with which God commands His people to care for those who desperately need provision and protection. Based on a wealth of vital but often over-looked Scriptural truth, this book is sure to surprise, challenge, empower, and ultimately bless you!"

—HEATHER KOPP, editor and bestselling author, and
—DAVID KOPP, co-writer of the *New York Times* bestselling,
The Prayer of Jabez and *Secrets of the Vine*

"Tom has produced an interesting and compelling work that I hope finds its way into the hands of every Christian who is asking, 'How can I make a difference for God in the world.' Through *Fields of the Fatherless* you will look into they eyes of some beautiful, but desperately needy children. Their stories will win your heart and through Tom's wise direction you will discover how to rescue their's. This book is on my 'highly recommended' list."

—CHUCK SMITH, JR.
Senior Pastor of Capo Beach Calvary and author of
The End of the World . . . As We Know It.

"Tom Davis has written a heart-stirring book that is sure to be a wake up call to all who desire to please God."

—LISA BEVERE
speaker and bestselling author of *Kissed the Girls and Made Them Cry*

"As taught in the book of James, religion that pleases God is caring for orphans and widows. Christ said, '...whoever gives to one of these little ones even a cup of cold water to drink, truly I say to you, he shall not lose his reward.' In this book, C. Thomas Davis explains the why and the how to, and he and the Lord give us great encouragement to do it. Enough said!"

—NORM MILLER
Chairman, Interstate Batteries

"C. Thomas Davis makes his case: We all can make a difference in the lives of the fatherless. What seems so daunting becomes so doable as Tom gently but insistently urges us to reach out to the lonely and the hurting—down the street and across an ocean. When we do just that, when we do reach out, our fear of getting involved with the fatherless quickly fades as we come to relish the privilege of reassuring young lives of our Father's unfailing love. Surely one reason Jesus taught us that it is better to give than receive is because, it turns out, giving is receiving."

—Dr. Mark Elliott, Director
The Global Center, Beeson Divinity School, Samford University

"The story of the fatherless causes such a kaleidoscope of deep emotions because it is our own story. Our home is Eden conversing with our Father, yet we all live far apart from the place and the parents we were designed for. Tom Davis provides us a mirror to our deepest pains and most powerful joys through the stories of amazing children and adults cared for by an even more amazing God. *Fields of the Fatherless* will move you to a life of deeper love and more urgent action."

—Brad Smith
President, Leadership Network

"Tom Davis has captured the essence of the gospel and our Christian social responsibility in eloquent tones. With so many people asking the question, 'What is God's will for my life?' it is important to remember the ethic of the gospel. Prisoners, widows and orphans are close to the heart of God. Tom reminds us that we cannot 'stand on the sidelines' but need to engage a needy world with the timeless truths of scripture. I wholeheartedly endorse his timely and direct message."

—Butch Maltby
President, Touchpoint Solutions

FIELDS
OF THE
FATHERLESS

Discover the Joy of Compassionate Living

C. Thomas
Davis

GLOBAL PUBLISHING SERVICES

For further information go to:
www.FieldsoftheFatherless.com
www.GlobalPublishingServices.com

❦ Dedication ❧

This book is dedicated to those God calls 'the fatherless,' whose cries are echoing across time, waiting for the ears of the church to hear. May their lives be radically changed because those calling upon the name of Christ as Savior hear their cries and are moved with compassion to act.

and

In Loving Memory to,

GERALDINE ALICE BRANHAM

Contents

⟡ Acknowledgements ⟡

There are some significant people, whose kindness and graciousness have greatly contributed to the birthing of this book. My heart is overflowing with thankfulness for their effort and encouragement.

Jason Milliken—this would never have been realized without you my friend. Thanks for you camaraderie and support. All we've ever talked about is just beginning. . . .

I would like to especially thank my project manager Katherine Lloyd who is a wonderful lady and a gift sent from above. Our relationship was divinely orchestrated, and hopefully will continue to be for years to come.

Eternal gratitude goes to my unsung hero, Heather Harpham Kopp, who personally sacrificed time and effort simply because she loved this project and has a huge heart.

Thanks to Holly Halverson for the hours of editing and reading that helped make this book a reality.

Without the inspiration of my good friend, Chuck Smith Jr., I'm not sure I'd have had the stamina to endure this undertaking. Thanks for your friendship and wisdom.

To my colleagues at Children's HopeChest who continually labor beside me in the fields of the fatherless, Rachel Andrews, Samantha Kerr, and Michele Davis, thank you. Visions aren't worth having if you see them alone.

To George Steiner, the president of Children's HopeChest, who believed in me, and continues to see things in me that are hidden to the rest of the world. A true man of God who is Christ-like in his every breath.

To Garrett Chynoweth for sharing this passion with me and helping bear the burden of what it means to enter the heart of God and live what He lives. You are truly a man who has lived this principle and made a difference in many fatherless lives.

To Simon Scionka for being a true-life companion. Sharing dreams with someone like you makes dreams worth having—za lubov.

Brandon Chynoweth, thanks for the initial inspiration and ideas you've shared. You're a true brother.

To the rest of my close family, Lisa, Calvin, Uncle Paul, and Tyler—you are all dear to my heart, and examples of God's overwhelming love to the fatherless.

Kevin Delp, thanks for being a friend who sees and inspires.

Thanks to Kevin and Jennifer Harrison who have a deep passion to make a significant difference in this world. They also reveal the true nature of Christ's character in their actions. Thanks for believing enough to sacrifice.

A special thanks to Pastor Lennie Allen for initially instilling in me a vision to reach the world and introducing me to the fields of the fatherless.

Dr. Tim Elmore, thank you for taking the time to help someone who had no idea what he was doing.

To my Grandfather, Herb Branham. Had you not taken in a little boy who desperately needed a father I would not be where I am today. Thanks for being my dad and for surrendering your retirement years to raise me. Your legacy will live on through my life and the lives of my children.

My life and this book would not have been complete without the loving support of my wife Emily. Sweetheart, you have truly been my source of inspiration and support. Thank you for giving me the confidence to be who God has called me to be. Thanks to the joys of my life, my neice Hannah and my wonderful children, Anya, Hayden, Gideon, and Scotlyn Grace, for being patient with your daddy while he was writing and you wanted to play!

In this world you are an orphan—

    eagerly anticipating your adoption as God's child.

In this world you are a widow—

    longing for reunion with your Bridegroom.

In this world you are a stranger—

    a pilgrim waiting to become a citizen of heaven.

And in this world, God has called you to care for the orphan,
the stranger, and the widow.

Fields of the Fatherless is a journey that brings you back
to what Christianity is really about:

    Giving yourself to others

        Being Christ to a hurting world

            And living for the one that comes next.

TREASURE
FOR THE TAKING

It happened on a brisk January day in 1947. In the Judean desert, several young Bedouin shepherds stared with searching eyes across the hills above the Dead Sea. One of their goats had gone astray somewhere along the height of those cliffs. The goat must be found! It would never last through the night with predators scouring the land in search of food.

The shepherds climbed to the place where they saw the goat last and discovered a number of caves—but no goat. They began to pick up rocks and throw them into the caves, one by one, in hopes of chasing out the lost animal. A strange cracking sound echoed from one of the caves. They looked at one another. What could be hidden in there?

Their hearts beat with excitement as they went inside. What they found was the greatest archaeological discovery of the twentieth century, the Dead Sea Scrolls. There were eight hundred different texts, roughly two hundred of them biblical and predating the earliest known Hebrew biblical texts by at least one thousand years.[1] The majority of these texts were not known to the world before. This was truly a monumental discovery!

Can you imagine, like these Bedouin shepherds, stumbling upon a priceless treasure in an abandoned cave or buried in an old, forgotten field? What sheer excitement and unspeakable joy!

This is exactly the feeling Jesus was trying to describe when He talked about the man who had found something wonderful in an unlikely place:

> *The kingdom of heaven is like a treasure hidden in a field, which a man found and hid; and for joy over it he goes and sells all that he has and buys that field.*
> (MATTHEW 13:44)

Did you catch that? It's because of abundant joy from the discovery that this man sells everything he has to obtain this treasure. Life suddenly takes on new meaning because of the knowledge and value of this find.

What I want to share with you is a truth "buried" in the
Word of God that He is earnestly waiting for you to come
upon. It has always been there, visible for anyone to see, yet
many of us have missed it. A lot of us just never saw it. Some
of us probably passed it by, not
realizing its worth. But far too few of
us actually possess the treasure I'm
talking about.

> Life suddenly
> takes on new meaning
> because of the
> knowledge and value
> of this find.

Think of this little book you're
holding as a treasure map that unlocks a marvelous treasure
chest of truth about what matters most to God—and should
matter most to us.

Maybe you're thinking, *Well, that's nice, Tom. I want to know
what God cares about. But where does excitement and joy come in?*

I think a lot of us have a very limited concept of joy—we
tie it to what makes us feel happy. But real joy goes even
deeper, and it's not always found in obvious places. Instead, it
hides in corners, waiting to be discovered when we sacrifice
our desires for God's desires.

For a long time, I missed the kind of joy I'm talking about.
Then I stumbled into some fields filled with treasure: the
Fields of the Fatherless. There I discovered what was really on

God's heart, and I was stunned. It changed my life forever.

I will explain more about these fields in the next chapter, but here I want to invite you to explore this treasure with me. I'm going to show you how caring for this group I call the *fatherless*—a passion so near and dear to God's heart—is a key to unlocking His blessing or His judgment.

Do you feel like your life is lacking? Have you been throwing rocks into a few caves in hopes of discovering something of value?

Did you hear that? The rock you just threw hit something, and there's a loud crash inside. . . .

Chapter One

WHAT ARE THE FIELDS OF THE FATHERLESS?

W *hat am I missing?*
   Some years ago, I found myself asking this
   question almost daily.

As a pastor, I thought I knew what mattered to God. I read my Bible almost every day. I tithed, I watched the "right" movies, I prayed as often as I could. And can you believe this— I kept my devotions more or less on track and I even journaled in an attempt to reflect on what was happening in my life!

But none of this could shake my conviction that there was a big chunk of the gospel I wasn't fulfilling.

The event God used to open my eyes was an overseas mission trip to Russia where I found myself among a group of orphans. I expected that with the depth of pain these kids had experienced in their short lives, they would be reserved with a complete stranger. I imagined them hiding in a corner, too afraid of people even to even say hi.

I was so wrong! These kids were so hungry for love and affection, as soon as our group made contact with them, we had what I call cling-ons—children who would "cling on" to us from that day forward!

During my time in Russia, God showed me two life-changing truths.

The first was how deeply in love He is with the poor and the outcast. Throughout my stay, I powerfully sensed God loving these kids *directly through me*.

The second truth was how much of God's joy could be mine when I participated with Him in doing something that mattered so much to Him! I had never before experienced God's pleasure and approval as strongly as I did in Russia.

And I had to know why.

That experience started me on a path of discovery in God's Word. It was a search that yielded surprising truths about the life God promises to bless—and about a special group of people.

The People on His Heart

If you searched the Bible from front to back, you'd find many issues close to God's heart. But you'd also notice three groups of people coming up again and again. They appear so many times, in fact, you have to conclude that God mentions them purposely to make sure they are at the top of our priority list.

> I experienced the pleasure of God in my every action when I was with those kids.

Allow me to introduce you to those God continually draws our attention to. They are the orphans, widows, and aliens (strangers). What these people have in common is their desperate need of provision and protection. They are the weak, the under-privileged, and the needy among us.

Scripture mentions the importance of caring for these individuals more than sixty times! Clearly, the protection and well-being of this group are one of God's great and constant concerns. So much so, in fact, He actually defines Who He is by His promises to them.

Consider His promise to provide:

> *A father of the fatherless, a defender of widows,*
> *Is God in His holy habitation.*
> *God sets the solitary in families;*
> *He brings out those who are bound into prosperity.*
> (PSALM 68:5–6)

His promise to ensure justice:

> *He administers justice for the fatherless and the widow, and loves the stranger, giving him food and clothing.* (DEUTERONOMY 10:17–18)

His promise to bless those who bless them:

> *At the end of every third year you shall bring out the tithe of your produce of that year and store it up within your gates. And the Levite, because he has no portion nor inheritance with you, and the stranger and the fatherless and the widow who are within your gates, may come and eat and be satisfied, that the Lord your God may bless you in all the work of your hand which you do.* (DEUTERONOMY 14:28–29)

Many other passages, including Isaiah 1:17, Psalm 82:3–4, and Zechariah 7:10, confirm God's commitment to this special group. They are the people on His heart. And they are the people He wants on our hearts, too.

It shouldn't surprise us that God would take direct action to ensure His intentions for the fatherless were carried out. The Bible reveals that God commanded His people to set aside a portion of their fields for the sole purpose of providing for this group. The line that designated this special area was called the "ancient boundary." It created a field, figuratively and literally, in which the fatherless, orphan, or widow could find the provision necessary to survive.

He actually defines Who He is by His promises to them.

We read about God's directives in Deuteronomy 24:19–21:

When you reap your harvest in your field, and forget a sheaf in the field, you shall not go back to get it; it shall be for the stranger, the fatherless, and the widow, that the Lord your God may bless you in all the work of your hands. When you beat your olive trees, you shall not go over the boughs again; it shall be for the stranger, the fatherless, and the widow. When you gather the grapes of your vineyard, you shall not glean it afterward; it shall be for the stranger, the fatherless, and the widow.

This boundary was so important, if you violated it, you transgressed against God:

> Do not move an ancient boundary stone,
> or encroach on the fields of the fatherless.
> For their Defender is strong;
> He will take up their case against you.
>
> (PROVERBS 23:10–11 NIV)

God established the fields of the fatherless so that any widow, orphan, or stranger in the vicinity of God's people would be provided for. Remember, this was an agrarian society. People lived and died based on their ability to farm the land. It was necessary to grow enough food to live off of for the spring and summer, along with a surplus to survive the fall and winter. For many, their crops, olive trees, and grapes represented their livelihoods.

So when God commanded that every person set aside a portion of his or her fields for the widow, alien, and orphan, He was telling them to set aside a portion of all they had. And He made it clear this was not a suggestion, or even an act of charity! Instead, this portion *belonged* to these people.

Now it's time to ask the obvious question. What about today? Did God stop caring about this group with the dawn of industrialism? Does He still have "fields" to provide for those in need? And if so, what does He expect from His people in an age when few of us are farmers?

Pure Religion

It would be easy to decide that God's principle about a field for the poor is just a quaint, ancient tradition—irrelevant today. Yet we clearly see in the New Testament that God's passion for the poor, parentless, and alienated transcends time. And His words concerning those in need are every bit as urgent in the New Testament as the Old.

For example, Jesus said, "But when you give a feast, invite the poor, the maimed, the lame, the blind. And you will be blessed, because they cannot repay you..."

The apostle James told us that caring for orphans and widows is the very essence of religion:

> Pure and faultless religion is this: to look after orphans and widows in their distress."
> (JAMES 1:27 NIV).

Acts 6 records an incident that is a great example of the priority the people who comprised the church in the New Testament placed on taking care of the poor.

When the number of disciples was increasing, the Grecian

Does God still have "fields" to provide for those in need?

Jews among them complained against the Hebraic Jews because their widows were being overlooked in the daily distribution of food. So the Twelve gathered all the disciples together and said, "It would not be right for us to neglect the ministry of the word of God in order to wait on tables. Brothers, choose seven men from among you who are known to be full of the Spirit and wisdom. We will turn this responsibility over to them and will give our attention to prayer and the ministry of the word."

This proposal pleased the whole group. They chose Stephen, a man full of faith and of the Holy Spirit, and six other men. They presented these men to the apostles, who prayed and laid their hands on them (from Acts 6:1–6 NIV).

What's important to note about this passage is that the apostles were the ones who were handing out the food! This was not a task to be swept under the table (no pun intended). Why? Because the apostles knew "pure religion" was ministering to those widows. They understood that such service was God's heart! At the point it became too overwhelming because of the numbers, they found men "full of faith and the Holy Spirit," laid hands on them, and appointed them to the task.

If the early church spent so much of its time focusing on the fatherless in this respect, shouldn't we make them a priority as well?

God gave the responsibility to care for the defenseless to those claiming to be followers of Christ. It is through our hands the Father's love comes, it is through our voices His voice is heard, it is through our efforts and those of the church that His care is revealed to the ones the rest of the world has forgotten.

> "Pure and faultless religion is this: to look after orphans and widows in their distress."

The Church in Action?

When you think about God's church, it is extremely important not to picture it as an institution surrounded by walls. The church consists of people who represent the physical body of Christ on the earth. We put flesh to His words and make Him alive to those who are desperate to know He is real.

Unfortunately, ministering in the fields of the fatherless hasn't been as much of a priority to the church in recent years as it has been throughout history. Today, many well-intentioned believers have lost sight of what God cares about most. The fact is, we put most of our energy into improving what is inside the four walls of our churches rather than bringing in the harvest that is outside.

A good friend once said to me, "If the fields are white for harvest, why do we spend all of our money on painting the barn?"

Ministry to Christ's body is important, but when we don't balance it with a legitimate attempt to care for the fatherless in our communities and around our world, something has gone dreadfully wrong.

The statistics reveal our neglect. There are more than 70 million orphans in the world. At least 35,000 children under the age of five die every day as a result of malnutrition or starvation, and there are at least one million children currently suffering under the oppression of forced prostitution. At least 100 million children are involved in child labor, and 1.5 million children are currently infected with AIDS.[2]

Yet, a 2001 Barna Research Group poll revealed a telling

statistic: evangelical Christians are less likely than are non-Christians to give money and assistance to AIDS-related causes. Only 3 percent of evangelicals say they plan to help with AIDS internationally as opposed to 8 percent of non-Christians.[3] This is only one example of how Christians have let down in their love for the unlovely.

It's not God's way. If we are to please Him, we must recover what has become a lost cause— the fatherless.

The encouraging news is, loving a person in need is much easier to do than you might think. It doesn't mean you have to become a missionary or take a vow of poverty! In some very practical ways, you can participate in the lives of those God is so passionate about and make differences that will last an eternity.

"If the fields are white for harvest, why do we spend all of our money on painting the barn?"

As you meet the fatherless in these pages, you will be surprised at how simple it is to make a dramatic change in a human life. You will learn how you can give just a little bit of God's love to someone else, and watch him or her transform. Abundant joy will be the result. As well as something you might not have anticipated...

The Promise of Blessing

None of us should ever care for the fatherless because of what we would get in return. This isn't about a 401K or an investment program! Yet a valuable blessing is in store for those of us who actively care for the fatherless.

Remember the passage in Deuteronomy 24?

> *When you reap your harvest in your field, and forget a sheaf in the field, you shall not go back to get it; it shall be for the stranger, the fatherless, and the widow, that the Lord your God may bless you in all the work of your hands.*

On the other hand, for the ones who choose not to heed God's message, a curse waits just around the corner: "Cursed is the one who perverts the justice due the stranger, the fatherless, and widow" (Deuteronomy 27:19).

The blessing of the Lord was not something the Jewish people took lightly. Many times, God's blessing enabled them to defeat their enemies. It was His kindness that prospered them and formed them into a great and mighty nation. The blessing of the Father meant the difference between success and failure, prosperity and poverty, abundance and want.

Carrying this understanding into the New Testament, the blessing of the Lord is something we are called to pursue because it is rightfully our inheritance:

> *Finally, all of you be of one mind, having compassion for one another; love as brothers, be tenderhearted, be courteous; not returning evil for evil or reviling for reviling, but on the contrary blessing, knowing that you were called to this, that you may inherit a blessing.*
>
> (1 PETER 3:8–9)

In both the Old and New Testaments, this word *blessing* connotes an infinitely lovelier circumstance than our word happiness. Happiness is related to luck or chance. It's a gambler's paradise. But the biblical word for blessing has to do with significantly satisfying fruitfulness. It relates to the roses around your lawn, the beauty of fresh-fallen snow on the mountainside, and spontaneous blasts of joy. God's blessing is not just a nice thing to have, it's a necessity for those who desire to walk in genuine satisfaction.[1]

The Hebrew word for "blessing" is *baruch*. It implies

being hunted down and pursued by the favor of the Lord. That is how much God desires for His people to be blessed!

> When we pay attention to the treasures of God's heart, we put ourselves in a position of blessing.

The blessing God poured upon His people was one that affected "all the work of [their] hands." It meant not only favor for the nation, but also favor for the individual.

In the same way, today God promises that if we take care of the needs of the fatherless, whatever we put our hand to will be blessed: our work, the home we build, and the relationships we hold, even the families we lead. When we pay attention to the treasures of God's heart, we put ourselves in a position of blessing.

I have personally seen this in action. From the moment we understood God's passion for the fatherless, my wife and I made it a priority to care for them. It never ceases to amaze me how God blesses our lives when we're ministering in these fields.

Let me give you an example. After doing what we could to help the fatherless by building relationships with kids from broken homes at our church and giving financially to some orphanages overseas, we decided to take our care one step further.

A little girl in a foreign country genuinely moved our hearts, and we decided to adopt her. There was one major problem: we didn't have the money to complete an adoption. Yet we felt we had a promise from God—He would provide. We knew His blessing rested on those who cared for the fatherless.

Two weeks before the adoption was final, we still didn't have the funds. Some days we were tempted to panic because time was short, but by the time we boarded the airplane to go pick up our new daughter, we had received more than ten thousand dollars from friends and others we didn't even know.

God always provides when we desire to help!

That's the provision of God in action. And it's part of the benefit that comes with ministry to the fatherless. God always provides when we desire to help! Proverbs promises that "he who has pity on the poor lends to the Lord, and He will pay back what he has given" (Proverbs 19:17).

A lifelong blessing will attach itself to your life when you follow the instructions of the Lord and join Him at work in His favorite fields.

Notes from the Field

I hated my life since the third grade when I was unmercifully beaten. I felt then that life is lost and death is looking for me. And my tears were telling me that life was nothing in comparison with death. I felt like a little cockroach, which [responds in] fear when seen.

A bunch of American people came to our school. I thought these people wanted to laugh at us. But I was mistaken. They are people willing to give up the most precious gift a person can possess, love. [Their] intentions to share seemed strange as they had their own kids. But these people have such big hearts to give that there is still enough room even for us little cockroaches.

Then I began to feel myself not a cockroach anymore which deserved to be killed, but a little human being. It is a wonderful feeling. Believe me.

—FROM A RUSSIAN ORPHAN

Chapter Two

THE FATHERLESS
OF TODAY

Jesus said we would always have the poor among us, so the question we need to answer is, who are the needy today? And how do we apply the ancient commands to twenty-first-century living?

I don't know about you, but I don't have a few hundred acres of farmland out back to share with the fatherless! What I do have is what those fields represent.

In a biblical culture, people lived by the sweat of their brow. As we saw in the last chapter, they made their living by growing grains, fruits and vegetables, as well as tending livestock. Today, our jobs and businesses are our livelihoods. They give us the harvest we have to share with the fatherless.

What do the fatherless look like today?

We can all picture the unforgettable sad-eyed orphans and the poverty-stricken Hatian kids with their stomachs distended, but what about those in our daily world?

Perhaps they look like...

- The widower at church who always shares candy with the squirrely kids...

- The girl who babysits your children and has no father at home...

- The single-mom next door who always seems to be harried—in and out of her car with kids, groceries, and work related paraphernalia...

- The unruly little boy at your child's class who keeps getting moved to another foster home.

- The lonely looking Asian college student waiting for the bus everyday as you pass by...

- Even your own grandma who lost her husband 10 years ago and spends her days watching soap operas...

It's More than Money

Right about now you might be thinking, "This book isn't for me! I don't have much money to give. I barely make ends meet as it is!"

Let me assure you that lack of funds doesn't disqualify you for service in God's fields! As you'll see in a moment, the care we're talking about goes way beyond money. Yet, too often I've noticed people using their own limited means as an excuse for doing nothing.

Another objection I often hear is this one: "Wasn't welfare created to help the poor?"

It's a fair question. But welfare is something that man's wisdom designed in an attempt to provide for those in poverty. Without getting into the dynamics of what problems the welfare system has generated, I think it's important to note that it is not a biblical idea.

Biblically, the needs of the poor were absorbed into society. After all, the needs of the fatherless aren't only financial, so throwing a check at the problem once a month isn't the answer. Their needs are also social, emotional and spiritual—needs money alone cannot solve.

And that's where you and I are supposed to come in.

> The needs of the fatherless aren't only financial, so throwing a check at the problem once a month isn't the answer.

Providing a portion of our fields involves our money, but it also means giving of our time to enter into the lives of the suffering in a way that makes a community and a family available to them.

Ruth and Boaz

Amazingly the Bible records a beautiful picture of this kind of broad redeptive caring that's as powerful as any contemporary example I could find. It's found in the book of Ruth, chapter 2.

Ruth and her mother-in-law, Naomi, are in a state of despair. Both are now widows, they are poverty-stricken and hungry. They decide to travel to the land of Naomi's ancestors, the Israelites. The problem here is that Ruth, a Moabitess is considered an enemy of the Jewish people and worshipper of other gods.

When they arrive, Ruth realizes their hope lies in a field of the fatherless. "Let me go to the fields and pick up the leftover grain behind anyone in whose eyes I find favor. . . . So she went out and began to glean in the fields behind the harvesters. As it turned out, she found herself working in a field belonging to Boaz . . ." (vs. 2-4).

How Boaz treats Ruth is a perfect picture of how God's people are to respond to the fatherless. Take a look at how the story unfolds:

Boaz takes special notice of Ruth working in his fields. He welcomes, affirms, and blesses her:

> The Lord repay your work, and a full reward be given you by the LORD God of Israel, under whose wings you have come for refuge" (vs. 12).

Boaz takes further steps to protect her. He tells her,

> . . . Do not go to glean in another field, nor go from here, but stay close by my young women. Let your eyes be on the field in which they reap, and go after them. Have I not commanded the young men not to touch you? (vs. 8-9A).

Boaz also provides for Ruth:

> And when you are thirsty, go to the vessels and drink from what the young men have drawn" (vs. 9B).

Then Boaz honors her by inviting her to his table.

> Now Boaz said to her at mealtime, 'Come here, and eat of the bread, and dip your piece of bread in the vinegar.' So she sat beside the reapers, and he passed parched grain to her; and she ate and was satisfied, and kept some back" (vs. 14).

Boaz is sensitive to the position she is in and respects her:

> He tells his men, "Even if she gathers among the
> sheaves, don't embarrass her. Rather, Pull out some
> stalks for her from the bundles and leave them for her
> to pick up, and don't rebuke her" (vs. 15).

And finally, the ultimate honor, Boaz makes Ruth part of his family,

> So Boaz took Ruth and she became his wife."
>
> (RUTH 4:13)

Each step Boaz made toward Ruth is the epitome of how Christ wants to appear to the world! Creating a path for us to follow, let's see how God manifested his unconditional love through Boaz:

- *He treated her with respect even as He acknowledged her need*— Today's poor feel embarrassed, down-trodden, maybe even bitter. They need to be treated as equals.
- *He provided for her*—No one should be without adequate food, shelter, and clothing. These basic necessities give a person worth so they can be open to receiving the love

God has for them. As God directs, we make our "fields" available as resources we can provide from.

- *He affirmed her*—The fatherless have lives that have been lanced with the pain of rejection and the anxiety of loss. A kind, affirming word will remind them of their value and has the same result as pouring water on dry, thirsty land.

- *He protected her*—Protecting people in need means to be an advocate for them. Stepping in to meet a need is a form of protection—just being a friend gives the assurance of protection from loneliness, hunger, fear.

- *He honored her*—What a statement it makes to invite a person in need to sit at your table and treat them as family.

- *And finally, the ultimate redemption—he made her family*— Redemption means salvation, deliverance, and rescue. We become part of helping restore right relationships with God.

As a picture of Jesus, Boaz embodies how we are to respond to the fatherless. As we welcome the lonely and needy to our tables, offer them respect, protection and provision, they will see Jesus and become part of our family—the family of God!

Job, one of the most righteous men who ever lived, committed his life to share what he had with the fatherless. When he asserted his integrity before God, he described the big picture of what we should all hope to achieve for those in need:

> If I have denied the desires of the poor
>
> or let the eyes of the widow grow weary,
>
> if I have kept bread to myself,
>
> not sharing it with the fatherless—
>
> but from my youth I reared him as would a father,
>
> and from my birth I guided the widow—
>
> if I have seen anyone perishing for lack of clothing,
>
> or a needy man without a garment,
>
> and his heart did not bless me
>
> for warming him with the fleece from my sheep,
>
> if I have raised my hand against the fatherless,
>
> knowing that I had influence in court,
>
> then let my arm fall from the shoulder,
>
> let it be broken off at the joint.
>
> For I dreaded destruction for God,
>
> and for fear of his splendor I could not do such things.
>
> (JOB 31:16–23 NIV)

Job's everyday life illustrated how to make sure the fatherless received what they needed—from fair treatment in court to clothing to fatherly guidance!

And isn't it interesting that when God talks about this group, He repeatedly uses the term "justice?"

> The sure way to deprive the poor of the justice due them is to do nothing.

In the last chapter we read that God commands us not to "distort the justice due an alien, orphan, and widow" (Deuteronomy 27:19 NASB). But what is the justice due to them? What rights do they have, and what provision can they expect from those who claim to be God's followers?

The truth might surprise you. You see, God doesn't consider our caring response to the plight of the needy as optional or as nice gesture. In fact, He sees a loving response to this group as a complete and pre-ordained human right—a legal right backed not by an earthly court but by the very halls of heaven!

So to deprive the fatherless of justice doesn't simply mean that you deny them a proper hearing in court. It means *not* welcoming them into your home, *not* helping them when they are cold and hungry, *not* listening when they cry out. In other words, the sure way to deprive the poor of the justice due them is to do nothing!

The apostle John goes so far as to suggest doing nothing is proof that God's love doesn't abide in us:

> But whoever has this world's goods, and sees his brother in need, and shuts up his heart from him, how does the love of God abide in him? (1 JOHN 3:16–17)

And James says if we see someone in need and give only lip service to caring for him or her, our faith is worthless:

> What does it profit, my brethren, if someone says he has faith but does not have works? Can faith save him? If a brother or sister is naked and destitute of daily food, and one of you says to them, "Depart in peace, be warmed and filled," but you do not give them the things which are needed for the body, what does it profit? Thus also faith by itself, if it does not have works, is dead. (JAMES 2:14–17)

I honestly believe when you strip Christianity down to its basics, this is what it means. To feed, clothe, and treat the fatherless as members of one's own family is to live out the call of Jesus Christ.

How do we do this? In chapter 4, I'll give you some very practical ways to jump in to the lives of the needy that will serve as a springboard to God's blessing.

Here, meet a few of the fatherless who found God's love through His followers.

The Fatherless Among Us

Emily

In her early childhood, Emily had everything most of us could ever want: a loving mother, a picture-perfect father, a beautiful home in an upper middle class neighborhood, five brothers and sisters with whom to love and fight with and make lasting memories. Emily had no warning life would deal her a devastating blow.

June 27, 1988, began like any other morning. Emily was only twelve years old. Another month, and she would join the ranks of the other proud teenagers of the world. The kids were out for summer vacation, so this would be another day of hanging out with friends and running through the water sprinklers somewhere in the neighborhood in order to get some relief from the humid south Texas heat. Dad was off to work and Mom was running errands with the younger ones, while the older kids tackled a new adventure for the day.

Later that morning, a man walked into the family-owned appliance shop. He shot Emily's father multiple times. It was a hate crime, committed by a member of the extended family, that took away the life of a loving father long before it was his time.

Unfortunately, this was only the beginning. The nature of the crime and the murderer behind it meant the family had to enter the witness protection program. They took assumed names and moved to California, away from friends, family, and everything they knew as home.

After this series of traumatic events, Emily's mother, Lillian, became extremely distraught and

> She desires to help others realize their tremendous value to their true Father.

spiraled into a deep state of depression. She was admitted to a psychiatric hospital while a friend tended the children. After undergoing intense counseling and treatment, this young mother of six was released from the hospital.

What the hospital staff failed to tell anyone in the family was that Lillian was on heavy doses of medication that could result in severe mood swings. Early the morning after Lillian came home, Emily woke to the sound of a gunshot. She ran into the living room with one of her brothers and discovered their mother's lifeless body lying on the living room floor.

Now all six of them were orphans, left alone in the world to fend for themselves. Emily, Brandon, Lisa, Garrett, Hannah, and Calvin were now sojourners in the fields of the fatherless.

Fortunately, a couple named Bob and Phyllis adopted all six of them and kept them together as a family. God's grace has been clearly revealed in the lives of these kids because a couple stepped out of their normal comfort zone and ministered the love of God to wounded children. And they are all changed forever because people cared.

I know all this firsthand because Emily is my wife. Instead of being bitter about her past, Emily is one of the most loving people I know. She continually sacrifices her time and resources to support the fatherless. Do you want to know why? Because she has been fatherless. And she knows the life-change that occurs when love is given. Her own loss helps her be responsive to others in similar situations. She desires to help them realize their tremendous value to their true Father.

Tom

I, too, have been one of the fatherless. I met my real father only a few times during the first sixteen years of my life. My mother married the proverbial "wicked stepfather," who was a career military man with a strong love for the bottle and not much else. When I was eleven, my mother decided to leave my step-father for the fifth of seven times. I had been attending a little church in town and was involved in the jr. high youth group.

Honestly, I attended church more to get away from the house once a week than I did to learn about God. I would have done just about anything to get out of the hellish home environment—it was that miserable of a place. But God pulled a fast-one on me. He used a painful time in my life to reveal His love for me through someone's caring concern.

I had nobody else to turn to with the circumstances facing me, so I told the youth pastor, Kurt. I didn't even know him very well. To my surprise he responded with a huge amount of love and affection! He offered to pick me up on the next Saturday to take me to eat, and to the park with his family. I became a member of his family for a day.

And what a day it was! I never felt so loved, so cared for, and like I actually mattered. I certainly didn't feel that way living in the place I was forced to call home. Our "family times" were daily events like drinking, cussing, yelling, and various forms of physical and verbal abuse. I lived with that menu for breakfast, lunch, and dinner. I could count on it.

But on that special Saturday Kurt treated me like his own child. He took me on a picnic, bought me ice cream, played soccer with me. Those acts of kindness were simple, but they made a profound impact on a needy child. He had absolutely nothing to gain personally. He just poured out biblical, selfless love to a little boy who desperately needed it. I had never felt such genuine love from anyone in my entire life. That experience changed me!

My mother and I packed up everything we could into a motor home and left early that following Monday morning.

> God used a painful time in my life to reveal His love for me through someone's caring concern.

I ended up in Midland, Texas, living with my grandparents.

A few short weeks later I found myself in another church, hearing the message of Christ's love. I gave my life to Him. I determined, if the love Christ had for me felt anything like the kind of love Kurt and his family gave me, I certainly wanted more of it—every day for the rest of my life.

Though I wasn't an actual orphan, I sure felt like one. I was desperately lonely and I felt as if nobody really loved me. My own family made me the object of their anger and aggression instead of their love. But on that Saturday, I was the happy recipient of the kind of love that is the most powerful. I experienced what real love felt like. I was hooked.

It was the kind of love that changes a life.

Angie

Angie is a single mother of three. Like thousands of other women across the country, she is the victim of several men who told her they loved her, then abandoned her after the birth of their child. Now Angie is left alone to raise these children with no help from the men who are supposed to be their fathers.

The needs she has to provide for on her own are overwhelming. Medical bills, child care while she works, rent, food, clothing, a car payment, gas—anyone can see this is an enormous burden for one person to handle.

Angie's life dramatically changed when a few people made the decision to respect her and love her unconditionally. Her story is a beautiful example of the church being Jesus: people gave money to help furnish her apartment, provided bags and bags of groceries, stepped in to watch the kids so she could go to work or just take a break. It was the kind of love that changes a life.

Because of their help, Angie went to Bible school and got a job teaching kids how to be gymnasts. She is also heading up a ministry to help others in the neighborhood the way she was helped! Because of those who stepped in to walk in the fields of the fatherless, Angie has come to know Jesus and to share His love with others. Just as Ruth was redeemed from her past, Angie has exchanged her burdens for freedom.

Think about the kind of impact it makes in the life of a fatherless person who has virtually nobody to love him, when someone like yourself reaches out with the love of Christ. Think about the boy or girl in your neighborhood who is a member of a single-parent home who may need the love you have to give. Think about the widow at church who may need your financial aid or the warmth of a family.

Your love in a fatherless person's life has the ability to transform his or her current reality and eternity. It did for me. That's why treating the fatherless like a member of your own family is so important to God. It's the only way they'll ever know His love for them: through you.

The Inspiration: Gratitude

Yet another principle revealed in Deuteronomy 24 is the issue of thankfulness.

> *Remember that you were slaves in Egypt, and the LORD your God redeemed you from there. That is why I command you to do this."* (DEUTERONOMY 24:18 NIV)

In other words: *Remember where you came from.* The idea of 'remembrance' was embedded deep in the Jewish culture. For example, Passover, was an event celebrating Israel's redemption from slavery in Egypt. Every time a Jewish family sat down for Passover, they were 'remembering' where they came from and how God had delivered them.

"Freely you have received, freely give."

Can you remember what it was like to not know the peace of God—to face your days alone? Remember when you didn't have that reassurance of salvation—when there was no hope for eternity? Remember how the Lord found you, had mercy on you and saved you.

As Peter reminds us, there was a time when you and I were not the people of God, before we found his love. Our gratefulness can be a wellspring that pours out the same kind of freedom and joy to others:

> But you are a chosen generation, a royal priesthood, a holy nation, His own special people, that you may proclaim the praises of Him who called you out of darkness into His marvelous light; who once were not a people but are now the people of God, who had not obtained mercy but now have obtained mercy.
>
> (1 PETER 2:9–10)

It is essential for us to feel the gravity of this kind of love and forgiveness, because it is out of this understanding we are to be merciful toward others: "Freely you have received, freely give" (Matthew 10:8). It is because of Christ's love for us, the fact that He forgave us such an enormous debt we could never pay, that we can show others the forgiveness and love of Christ.

Genuine, believing faith manifests itself in tangible ways when we care for those who are poor, suffering, and those without father or mother. Your own gratitude makes you sensitive—you can't help but feel compassion and act on it.

> *The man whith two tunics should share with him who has none, and the one who has food should do the same."* (LUKE 3:11 NIV)

This is how the Lord provides for the needy within the community of faith. What we have received in abundance we are to pass along. Think about what you can share with the fatherless today.

Notes from the Field

I was a single mom needing to move to another town for job reasons, but I couldn't afford to hire professional movers. I knew I couldn't possibly load and unload a U-Haul by myself.

Yet I couldn't bring myself to ask friends for help. After all, everyone knows what kind of hard work and hassles moving involves.

A couple weeks before the move, I bumped into a friend who knew of my plans. When she offered to help, I assumed she was just being polite. "Well, maybe. I'll let you know..."

But she insisted. "My boyfriend and I are going to help you move next Saturday."

"Really?" I asked.

She said, "Yes, we are." Just like that. Later that week she called to ask what time they should come over on the day of the move.

My friend's decisiveness was just what I needed. Often people don't realize how hard it is for single moms who need help to ask for it—and even to receive it when it's offered! Thank you dear friends for insisting, and for taking the time out of your own busy Saturday. I'm learning that there are people who truly want to help and I'm discovering I can let them.

—Single mom, Oregon

Chapter Three

EVER WONDER WHAT GOD LOOKS LIKE?

I s it possible for a man or woman to look into the face of God and live? Historical accounts in the Bible tell us that only one man was privileged to actually see God. In Exodus we find out God spoke with this man "face to face, as a man speaks to his friend" (Exodus 33:11). The inevitable result: he was distinctly marked forever. His name was Moses.

The effect of actually being in God's manifest presence was powerful—it literally changed Moses' physical appearance. His face was shining so brightly, he had to put a veil over it. The glory of God was so strong, the people couldn't bear to see it.

In the New Testament, things change considerably. God became man, took up His residence in human flesh as Jesus, and came to live among us. The mystery of all mysteries! As 100 percent human and 100 percent God, Jesus Christ walked on this earth. Mankind was finally able to see God face-to-face, and those who saw Him were, like Moses, marked forever. As Jesus said, "He who has seen Me has seen the Father" (John 14:9 NASB). Seeing God by being with Jesus—what an incredible gift!

Have you ever had a spiritual event occur in your life that was so real, so dramatic, it changed who you are and how you live? One of those defining moments in time where you knew you touched the eternal?

I remember such an event when I was in high school. It wasn't even the "happening" that was so profound, it was the message it brought me.

I finally had what every sixteen-year-old dreams of: the coveted driver's license. I waited all of my life for this! Although the car my grandfather bought wasn't exactly the car of my dreams—a fifteen-year-old Buick Regal with a second-rate paint job—at least it ran! But most important, I was now behind the wheel.

One horribly humid Texas summer day, I was on my way to golf practice. I lived with my grandparents in a fairly affluent community where neighbors were usually extremely helpful to one another. But on this day, everyone's southern hospitality must have just been played out.

As I turned a corner, I saw some sort of commotion about a half-mile ahead of me on the side of the road. An older lady was standing by her car, trying to flag someone down. The two cars in front of me drove right past as if they saw nothing. But I pulled over.

I got out of my car and realized what this lady was so frantic about. She had been trying to get her very elderly mother out of the car and into

> God became man, took up His residence in human flesh as Jesus, and came to live among us.

her wheelchair, when the attempt went haywire and her mother fell over into the yard. The poor lady was lying along the side of the road with the wheelchair on top of her. Several attempts by her daughter to get her back into her chair had failed miserably.

I helped the kind, elderly lady who was about to hyperventilate because she was so upset. I picked her up off of the ground, got her into the chair and safely into her house.

Those two ladies were so thankful! They thought I was the most darling young man around and were ready to nominate me for Citizen of the Year. The daughter told me they had been there for over thirty minutes, trying to get someone to pull over and help them. Everyone was just too busy.

Well I left there feeling on top of the world! I had done something to help someone in need; in fact, someone who was entirely helpless without my assistance. And for some reason, I felt like I had done something special to please the heart of God—He was smiling at me and enjoyed my meager efforts.

> I left there feeling on top of the world! I had done something to help someone who was in need.

I think for the first time in my life I had an encounter where I saw the face of God. I did—I saw it in that elderly lady who was lying on the ground in need of someone to show some compassion. That's why I felt the way I did. My actions that day thrust me into the realm of the eternal. I had met Jesus in a way I never thought about.

Jesus Is Very Near

You may be wondering, *How could you possibly see the face of God in an elderly lady on the side of the road?* Allow me to explain. Or better yet, let Jesus explain.

In Matthew 25, Jesus gives a remarkable picture of what the end of the world will be like, and what will happen at the judgment. In doing so, He reveals how important our actions on this earth are and how they will affect our eternity. Beginning in verse 31, Jesus comes in all of His glory to separate the sheep from the goats—the true believers from the false believers. After the division, He tells the sheep—the true believers—to enter the kingdom of God He has prepared for them since the beginning of the world. And then He tells them why they are able to enter:

> For I was hungry, and you gave Me something to eat;
> I was thirsty, and you gave Me drink; I was a stranger,
> and you invited Me in; naked, and you clothed Me;
> I was sick, and you visited Me; I was in prison, and you
> came to Me. (MATTHEW 25:35–36 NASB)

The righteous are confused. They can't think of a time when they did any of this directly to Jesus. How can you minister to Jesus and miss it? His answer is in verse 40: "I tell you the truth, whatever you did for one of the least of these brothers of mine, you did for Me (NIV)."

Now their eyes are opened. When the righteous gave to others, they were giving to Jesus. Wow! *If that's the reason Jesus gives for ushering us into His kingdom, it is surely a powerful statement as to what He's looking for from us.*

It's interesting that those mentioned weren't the upper class of society, they were the down and out. They were those who couldn't care for themselves, the helpless, the needy. Ministering to these people, Jesus said, is equal to ministering to Him.

In a very vulnerable way, this reveals the heart of our Lord. He aches for those in pain, He sees the needs of the hungry and hungers with them, He hears the cry of the orphans, identifies Himself with their misery, and lowers Himself to their level.

> "Whatever you did for one of the least of these brothers of mine, you did for Me."

In his book *Something Beautiful for God*, Malcolm Muggeridge gives us a meaningful picture of what this service looks like in one of us. His example was the late Mother Teresa, who unarguably gave her life to loving the people Jesus loved most. He described her as a woman . . .

. . . with this Christian love shining about her; in her heart and on her lips. Just prepared to follow her Lord, and in accordance with His instructions, regard every derelict left to die in the streets as

Him; to hear in the cry of every abandoned
child, even in the tiny squeak of the
discarded fetus, the cry of the Bethlehem
child; to recognize in every leper's stumps
the hands which once touched sightless eyes
and made them see, rested on distracted
heads and made them calm, brought health
to sick flesh and twisted limbs.[1]

This is a key to understanding the passage of Jesus as
suffering servant in Philippians 2:

> *[Jesus,] who, being in the nature God,*
> *did not equate equality with God something to be*
> *grasped, but made himself nothing,*
> *taking the very nature of a servant. . . .*
> *He humbled himself, and became obedient*
> *to death—even death on a cross!*
>
> (PHILIPPIANS 2:6–8 NIV)

Jesus, in order to reveal His love to creation left the beauty
and perfection of heaven to be identified with all people.

In other words, He emptied Himself of all that He was, in order to be one of us. In all our filth, all our sin, all our weakness, He became part of humanity—became our brother. You see, we *all* are the least of these!

We have a tendency to look at passages like this in the Bible and say, "Oh, those poor dears, hungry, thirsty, sick, and needy." But that's the great paradox! That's exactly who we were before Jesus found us! We are all the same at the core. And because He has poured out such love and care for us, we are to go find "the least of these," and do the same.

The truth is, we see Jesus in the eyes of the poor *because we see in them who we really are.* We are able to have genuine compassion as Christ has compassion on us— because we see ourselves.

> He left the beauty and perfection of heaven to be identified with all people.

One last thought. Remember how in the beginning we spoke of the joy that occurs when we participate in helping those who God cares about most? I'd like to think about that again for a minute.

You may be saying, "I would love to help the fatherless, but it is so heartbreaking!" You know, true joy doesn't always come through the things that give us the warm fuzzies.

Despite what Jesus knew he would have to go through dying on the cross, he trusted in what God wanted him to do. He saw the bigger picture. It's difficult to grasp, but the reward that will come far outweighs any of the uncomfortable feelings we may have. So we . . .

> . . . *fix our eyes on Jesus, the author and perfecter of faith,* who for the joy *set before Him endured the cross, despising the shame, and has sat down at the right hand of the throne of God* (emphasis mine).
>
> HEBREWS 12:2 (NASB)

Did you see that?! For *the joy* he knew was coming, he gave himself. That's our example. As we focus on fulfilling what is on God's heart, looking ahead to the joy He promises—we help others find the love of God through the giving of ourselves. That's the ultimate goal!

God's Face Today

So what does God look like?

He looks a lot like that orphan in Romania who doesn't have a hope in the world unless someone like you or I enters his life and reveals to him the love of the Father.

He looks like that little girl in Africa who has no father, who has watched her mother's body be ravaged by AIDS for the last five years, and has been crying over and kissing her since she took her last breath about ten minutes ago. Now she has nobody, she's only seven, and she's standing all alone on a dirt road as they carry her mother away.

Oh, look! Another glimpse of God. He looks like the struggling single mother you know who is hanging on by an emotional thread. She is mother, father, protector, and provider, and to top it all off, she has to leave the child she loves so much in the hands of a stranger all day, just so she can put food on the table.

Oh, look! Another glimpse of God. This time in the eyes of that young Palestinean student who just left his entire family to study in America. He's all alone, a stranger, and in need of someone to show him what the real love of God feels like.

Yes, Jesus looks a lot like those people. Will you look for His face in all of the others you see today?

Right now Jesus is hungry. Jesus is thirsty. Jesus is naked. Jesus is in prison. Jesus is sick. Will you do what it takes to minister to Him? For the joy set before you . . . search for the treasure in earthen vessels . . . and you'll find Christ Himself.

Notes from the Field

It always puts a smile on my face to think of the days when I met you. Most of all I remember the moment when you told us about the Lord. I know if He helped you, He will help me too.

I was put in the foster care system when I was three. Everyone loved me when I was small. I took joy in life. Then the years started going faster and faster. I was a big girl already. Good days are always over at some point. Everyone left me, my brothers, my sisters. I was left alone. Then my life stopped. I kept seeing my relatives in my dreams. I quit sensing, playing the guitar, everything. But then you came into my life. When you told me about Jesus I came back to life...I think God will help me to find my sister. I pray He'll help me to get to know Him better...

Love, Katie

—From a young girl in foster care

Chapter Four

SEEDS
OF HOPE

Take a moment to consider the lowly seed. One of the most amazing things about a seed is the mystery of how something so small and insignificant can turn into something so big, beautiful, and full of life.

My boys and I contemplated this a few days ago. We live in Colorado, and the growing season in this part of the country is very short, to say the least. As we were enjoying a rare seventy-two-degree day, my boys and I took on the tricky task of April seed planting in Colorado.

They couldn't believe how tiny the seeds were! My oldest son said to me, "Dad, that seed is so small, nothing could grow from it. I can't even see it to plant it in the soil!" What a perfect time for a father to teach his son about how something inconspicuous can turn into something great; how just a little effort of planting in the spring can bring a wealth of flowers to enjoy all summer long, along with tomatoes, cantaloupe, and other yummy things to eat. My son is still having a hard time believing those seeds will actually turn into those things, but he says he'll take my word for it.

The Power of Planting Seeds

Many of the significant outcomes in our lives are the result of someone planting a seed. It was a seed that started your life and has grown, produced fruit, and made you into the person you are today.

Think of the things that would never exist if someone hadn't started the process. Every beautiful piece of art, every major historical monument, the homes we live in, and everything man has created started with the seed of a small thought and grew into reality.

One of the most significant seeds we can ever plant—especially in the life of someone who is fatherless—is the seed of hope. A field has no hope of a future crop without the planting of a seed. Hope is vital to every person's survival, especially when the odds are completely against him.

A true story told in Ken Gire's book, *The Weathering Grace of God* made an impact on me relating to the power of planting seeds.[4]

It comes from a man named Jean Giono, who tells of his encounter with a shepherd in the French Alps. At the time, deforestation had almost completely destroyed the land. The mountains and valleys were barren, the wildlife had deserted the area in search of greener pastures, and villagers had abandoned their homes because their springs and brooks had run completely dry.

> Something so small and insignificant can turn into something big, beautiful, and full of life.

While mountain climbing in this ravished area, Giono came to a shepherd's hut, where he was invited to spend the night. During their conversation, he learned that the fifty-five-year-old shepherd, Elzeard Bouffler, had been planting trees on the barren hillsides for more than three years. That evening Giono watched Bouffler meticulously sort through a large pile of acorns and pick out one hundred of the best seeds. It was a rather mundane task nobody would notice and even care about. Yet during those three years Bouffler planted 100,00 seeds, 20,000 of which had sprouted.

After World War I, Giono returned to the same mountainside where he had met the shepherd years earlier. The area looked entirely different. Where there was once a barren and deserted land were now the beginnings of a living, vibrant forest! A chain reaction in nature was occurring: water flowed in the once-empty brooks. Meadows, gardens, and flowers were birthed where once complete desolation ruled.

Giono again returned to the French Alps after World War II. This time he found the shepherd continued the thankless task twenty miles from the front lines. A vigorous forest, inhabited by farms and families, now covered the originally empty hillside. The beauty of the land had been restored for everyone to enjoy.

> Will you plant a seed of hope in lives that have been stripped bare by the misery of this world?

All of this took place because of the effort of one man planting seeds. Where everyone else saw stripped hillsides void of any value, a shepherd saw the hope of seeds being planted that would one day bring back the beauty and glory the land once possessed.

One person has the ability to completely revolutionize the life of an abandoned child, a foreigner who is here to study or to work, a single mom, or an elderly widow. Your creative energy could be the very thing that helps her or him keep going and even experience God's love for the first time.

The question is, will you be a seed planter? Will you just look at the devastation around you and find another place to make your home or will you plant a seed of hope in lives that have been stripped bare by the misery of this world?

When I'm Weak

Earlier I mentioned the staggering numbers of oppressed children in our world today. Here is another alarming statistic: The number of single-mother households with children under the age of eighteen has remained at 9.8 million since 1995. There are 11.6 million single-mother households with children under twenty-one. In 1998, 26 percent of all families with children were headed by single parents.[1]

And the result? "Almost 70 percent of young men in prison grew up without fathers in the home."[2]

The need to reach out to the alien or stranger in our country is also great: "A record total of 547,867 International Students on US campuses for the year 2000-2001. [In addition] enrollment rose 6.4 percent—the largest increase since 1980."[3]

That's just the number on campuses! Just think of how many others are here from foreign countries working or attending high schools on international exchange programs. The stranger is in our country, and in need.

It's clear that the fields of the fatherless are full to the brim with needy people. After reading these kinds of statistics, you may be asking, *What difference can I possibly make?* This was my question too. We're all concerned we don't have the resources, and we don't know where to start.

A rather old, quirky story has something to say about this issue.

A young man collecting seashells noticed an aged fellow walking along the beach. He saw this old man walk a few steps, bend over, pick something up, and fling it into the sea. He repeated this over and over.

Filled with curiosity, the young man moved closer until he realized what the old man was doing. He was picking up one of the many starfish that lay dying on the beach and throwing them far into the water.

The young man thought this task was an incredible waste of time. So he asked, "Sir, why are you taking the time to try to save one starfish when there are thousands lying on the beach? You can't possible make any difference!"

The older man smiled, bent over, picked up another starfish, and flung it into the ocean. Then he said, "It made a difference to that one!"

This simple illustration teaches us the importance of one action. We may not be able to do everything, to save all of the fatherless in the world—this I grant you. But all of us are able do *something* that can significantly alter the life of one person whom God loves and cherishes.

> We're all concerned that we don't have the resources, and we don't know where to start.

Feeling too weak to make a difference, too empty of resources, or too fearful to try is a normal human response. I'm so glad for promises like 2 Corinthians 12:9–10 that encourage us to continually trust in God for strength, We can rely on Him to use the impossible-looking situations to bring about the possible!

"My grace is sufficient for you, for power is perfected in weakness." Most gladly, therefore, I will rather boast about my weaknesses, that the power of Christ may dwell in me. Therefore I am well content with

weaknesses ... for Christ's sake; for when I am weak,

then I am strong.

Personal weakness provides a great opportunity for

> We can step out,
> believing in God's strength
> to help us, instead of
> letting our limitations
> defeat us.

God's strength to come through!
He's just waiting for us to call upon
Him in our weakness so He can
show Himself strong on our behalf.
What a great position to be in!

We need to change our minds about how we approach the
things we fear (more on this in the next chapter) and the places
in our lives where we feel weak. We can step out, believing in
God's strength to help us, instead of letting our limitations
defeat us. Then we can confidently join Paul and actually boast
in our weaknesses because that is when God is about to show
His power.

Every Seed Counts

I remember a real-life picture of a small seed of hope emerging.
I was visiting an orphanage and looking for a little friend I had
made at summer camp, Mark. Having been in almost every
nook and cranny of the orphanage trying to find him, I resigned

myself to the fact that he must be somewhere in the city. But then, hunched down in the corner of the last room I entered, I found Mark.

When I said his name, he looked up and I noticed two things. One, he had a nasty shiner on his left eye. Two, he was reading a Bible someone had given him at camp. We never did find out what happened to Mark's eye—he wouldn't say. But we did discover that, in spite of his current circumstances, Mark was finding comfort and solace in the Word of God that someone had given him.

That act—that seed—was a relatively easy and inexpensive thing to do. And there, right in the middle of the orphanage, a tree was sprouting and promising fruit that would last forever.

One day, there will be a forest grown in Mark's life, from a single seed planted by someone who took the time. Someone like you or me. Or George.

George's Story

There are many inspiring real-life examples men and women who have followed God's call and affected thousands! I think of the many heroes of faith throughout history who have changed the lives of so many. And those changes all started with one act of love that had a ripple effect on others. A modern-day hero of mine is George Steiner.

After the fall of Communism, there was an open door for Christian literature to be distributed in the orphanages. George was working in Russia with International Bible Society, distributing children's Bibles. What he saw there floored him! The kids were living in deplorable

> And there, right in the middle of the orphanage, a tree was sprouting and promising fruit that would last forever.

conditions. It was so cold you could see your breath in the orphanage. Many kids were sick because of malnutrition and they were starved for even a little love and affection. His burden was to help these children experience hope.

George learned some staggering facts about these kids after they no longer live at the orphanages. 60 percent of all girls leaving the orphanages would end up as prostitutes, 70 percent of the boys would end up on the streets or in jail, and 15 percent of the children would commit suicide within the first two years out on their own.[5]

After returning to the U.S., George felt he had to do something, anything, to help these kids. Because of the stage of life he and his wife were in, they couldn't adopt. But he asked God how he could be used to make a difference across the world in the lives of those who need so much?

George felt his greatest blessing from God was a strong, loving family. He finally realized what he could give—the seed he could plant—was a portion of the love he himself had received. Certainly he could do something to help provide for the orphans' basic needs—physical, emotional, and spiritual—in the same way he provided for his two daughters.

So that's what he began to do. He invested his time, his talent, and his treasure in helping orphans. He told many of his friends about his vision and together they started an organization called Children's HopeChest. Today, Children's HopeChest helps thousands of orphans across Russia and Romania on a daily basis, all because one man cared enough to take the little he had and give it to the fatherless.

Seeds for Today

Romans 12:1 encourages us to live a transformed life because of our commitment to God: "I beseech you therefore, brethren, by the mercies of God, that you present your bodies a living sacrifice, holy, acceptable to God, which is your reasonable service."

Being a living sacrifice starts with just being sensitive to those God brings to your attention—single moms, widows, foster kids, the homeless, and anyone you see hurting.

Here are some suggestions for ways to affect the lives of the fatherless:

- Call an organization that focuses on orphans and become a personal sponsor. You can pick the age and gender, and you will receive a short history on your child. Children's HopeChest is one such organization: 800-648-9575 or visit www.hopechest.org.

- Decide to befriend a child who is the member of a single-parent home. Many of these children are right under our noses. Find them. Take them out for a soda or to an amusement park or concert. Be a mom or dad, brother or sister, to them for just a day at a time.

- Help a single mother. We all know them. And most of them are doing everything they can to make a life for their family. Be a friend and help her! Watch her little ones once a week, help with groceries—be creative.

- Gather a small group of friends and commit to place a small amount of your income, maybe 1 or 2 percent, into a fund. Choose trustworthy organizations that are helping the poor and begin giving to a cause of your choice on a regular basis. You may decide to support a good friend on the mission field or give to specific projects overseas, but whatever you do, begin giving.

- Write letters to an orphan overseas. (Children's HopeChest can help with this.)

- Find a widow in your community and sacrifice some time for her. Mow her yard, run errands, or just invite her over for tea and visit with her. Be consistent in developing a relationship.

- When you hear of someone who is sick and doesn't have any family close by, be his or her family—if only for a day. Take the sick one balloons, a get-well card, or make a meal.

> Being a living sacrifice starts with just being sensitive to those God brings to your attention.

- Find out about foreign students who are attending your local university. A great organization to help you connect with foreign students is International Students Inc. Contact them by calling 1-800-ISI-TEAM or going to their website: www.isionline.org. Have a few of them over for dinner. Maintain contact with them and invite them to share the holidays with your family.

- Become a foster parent. Look in the community pages in your phone book for the program in your area. They have regular information meetings to help you find out about being a foster parent.

- During the holidays, adopt a needy family in your community. But this year, make it a point to continue the relationship with the family you choose to help.

- Instead of a family vacation to Hawaii this year, go on a mission trip. As a family unit, engage the fatherless and see not only what a change you'll make in their lives but what kind of miracles also happen in your family!

- Make it a point to befriend someone who lives in the inner city or "on the other side of the tracks." Expand your peer group beyond those of the same economic status as yourself.

> Simple acts of kindness are all it takes to change a life, a community, even a nation.

- Volunteer at a local soup kitchen or homeless shelter. Do more than serve food, show you care by lending a listening ear.

- Next time you're in a long line at the grocery store, genuinely smile at the lonely-looking person standing there too.

- If you're a male, organize a group of fellows to buy used cars, fix them up, and give them away to single moms and widows who need transportation.

In the days ahead, the seeds you plant will sprout. They will grow tall and bear fruit for God's kingdom. Life will return and replace the barrenness once found in hopeless hearts. And you may be a hero because you took the time to be involved.

Simple acts of kindness are all it takes to change a life, a community, even a nation.

Want to start your own forest today?

Notes from the Field

Finances is usually a big issue with us single moms. We struggle to make ends meet and I can't think of anyone who doesn't live payday to payday.

This summer was one of those times when I could actually breathe a sigh of relief about my money situation. I'd finally caught up, been able to pay all the minimum amounts due on my bills, and was just hoping nothing would derail me for at least a couple of months. Then poof! Within 2 days I did get derailed.

My son had an asthma attack and the co-pays on the appointment and medication totaled $80.00. Then the next morning I got a phone call from a bed & breakfast I'd booked months previous as a surprise birthday present. I had totally forgotten I'd made the reservation and they informed me that because I didn't show up they had to charge my debit card. An unexpected, wasted, $120.00! I was mad at myself, down, and discouraged. Sunday came and went and then on Monday morning I went

in to work and found a card on my chair.
I opened it and in it was $200.00 cash. The
card was one of encouragement, but with no
signature. I became sure it was no one from
work; they reported a female had dropped it
off—someone whom they didn't recognize.

What a blessing! And for exactly the same
amount I'd "lost." The fact that God would give
back even when I'd made the stupid mistake of
forgetting the reservation meant so very much
to me. I was so filled with joy at the thought of
it. Rather than let me live in the consequences
of my forgetfulness, He laid it on someone's
heart to give that much at that exact time.
It was a miracle.

Thank you—whoever you are—for listening
and being willing to be God's hands extended.

—WIDOW, MOM OF FOUR

Chapter Five

THE OLD ENEMY: FEAR

Have you ever wondered about the things that really drew Jesus' attention when He walked the earth? What was it, more than anything else, that stirred His heart and caused Him to stop what He was doing and act on the moment? It was another human being in need.

"And seeing the multitudes, He felt compassion for them, because they were distressed and downcast like sheep without a shepherd." (MATTHEW 9:36 NASB)

When Jesus noticed the defenseless, God's love was most tangible. Jesus identified with the ones who were forced to live in a perpetual state of misery and did something to relieve their pain. In Matthew 8 and Luke 17, He touched lepers and healed them when the rest of society declared them "unclean." In John 4, Jesus reached out to an adulterous woman in Samaria during a time when men weren't supposed to talk to women in public—especially women with questionable lifestyles. In Matthew 19, when the disciples were rebuking people for bringing their children to Jesus to bless, He stepped in saying, "Let the little children come to Me, and do not forbid them; for of such is the kingdom of heaven" (Matthew 19:14). This is what the character of our Savior is like.

> When Jesus noticed the defenseless, God's love was most tangible.

Compassion Equals Involvement

Let's talk about compassion for just a moment. Most of us would consider ourselves compassionate people, wouldn't we? In fact, *compassion* is one of those words that is supposed to characterize most everyone—especially in America. But if compassion and being a human being are one in the same, why is humanity so filled with hate, violence, war, and oppression? Why are so many around us suffering from hunger and poverty, and lacking the basic necessities of life? Why are millions of human beings trying to cope with feelings of isolation, alienation, and loneliness?[1]

Just looking at our world tells us that we have to rethink our understanding of compassion. What does it really mean to be compassionate, and how can we do this the way Jesus did? Is compassion merely showing kindness to those who are less fortunate than we are? Does it mean that in general, we don't inflict pain purposely on another? Is it occasionally sending money to a charity organization or donating some clothes to a homeless shelter? While small actions can and do produce results, I suspect compassion—the way Jesus practiced it—means a bit more than that.

I can't find a better definition of compassion than one given by Henri Nouwen:

> The word *compassion* is derived from the Latin words *pati* and *cum*, which together mean "to suffer with." Compassion asks us to go where it hurts, to enter into places of pain, to share in brokenness, fear, confusion, and anguish. Compassion challenges us to cry out with those in misery, to mourn with those who are lonely, to weep with those in tears. Compassion requires us to be weak with the weak,

vulnerable with the vulnerable, and powerless
with the powerless. Compassion means full
immersion in the condition of being human.[2]

There you have it. The definition of compassion is about
involvement. To be compassionate means to get out of the
boat of our current circumstances and get into the boats of
those who are suffering. We are called to bear the burdens of
those who are in need of our companionship—to "weep
with those who weep" (Romans 12:15). It's not exactly a
popular message.

You know, when we look at how Jesus responded, it's
almost as if the grimmer and more hopeless the
circumstance, the more attention He gave it.

Let's look at some examples:

In Luke 8, Jairus's only daughter—twelve years old—had
died. But Jesus went into the pain of his family and brought
about new life by raising her from the dead.

In Luke 9, a man begged Jesus to heal his son, telling
Him, "A spirit seizes him, and he suddenly cries out; it
convulses him so that he foams at the mouth; and it departs
from him with great difficulty, bruising him" (Luke 9:39).

Most of us would run from that kind of scene, but not Jesus. He walked into the distress, healed the man's son, and gave him back to his father.

Is this true for us? Are we drawn by the daily needs of those around us? Are our hearts moved by the emptiness we see in the eyes of a newly divorced young person? Do we recognize the pain of the business executive who has just been downsized into unemployment? Are we compassionate people? Does our compassion force us to act?

> "Compassion means full immersion in the condition of being human."

Most likely the hardest thing for us to be confronted with is the face of a fellow human being in desperation. I think of the countless times I have driven by a beggar on the side of the road or walked by a homeless person in a dark, dreary ally, never intending to lend a helping hand. Haven't you done that a time or two? In our minds, we walk through all of the reasons why we shouldn't help: "They would probably just use any money I gave them for drugs," or "You know, there are plenty of places for that person to get help if he wants it. He would just rather be a bum." But there isn't any compassion in those attitudes.

If we translate this to the needs we hear about in other

places around the world: Do we cry for the child in Honduras whose only source of sustenance is the trash heap he lives on? Does our soul ache for the infant who is abandoned on the side of a dirt trail in India, screaming for a meal from her mother, until she screams her last? Perhaps we don't react much to reports of those who are starving to death by the thousands, children living in the slums because they have no parents, young girls in Thailand sold into prostitution by their fathers for only a month's wage .

These needs seem remote, so removed from our lives. Most of us in the West can't even identify with such suffering, much less think of ways to help. So, much of the time, we do nothing. Don't we all felt the shame and guilt of wanting to help, but when it comes time to act we just can't pull it off? Something stops us from digging down inside of our soul and mustering up whatever it takes to move us to action.

The Padlock on Our Compassion: Fear

There's a common, very human reason for our resistance. You see, the reason we don't help the beggar on the road, or the single mother we know who is working herself to death, is the same reason we won't help the orphan dying on the other side of the world. We flee from the need in front of us because of our ancient, ruthless foe, *fear.*

When we see or hear about the atrocities happening to children in America or other countries, the fear of our lives being rudely interrupted enters into the equation of our attempts to help. We think, *What if I became too involved?*

We are afraid of changing what we've always done. Our lives have become comfortable and manageable. If loving the stranger, the widow, and the poor have never been a part of our lives in the past—even if we know it should be—it's much easier to keep on living the way we always have.

> Something stops us from digging down inside of our soul and mustering up whatever it takes to move us to action.

I've known so many people who feel they are called to give up their present lifestyle and follow Christ in missions or youth ministry or other service. But they're just too afraid.

And others are intimidated by little things God asks them to do like becoming a volunteer helper at a week-long summer daycamp for kids.

The idea may cross our minds to sign up to bring a meal to the older widow who broke her hip last week. But then maybe we rationalize our lack of follow-through by telling ourselves someone else will do it.

What if these impulses are from God? What kind of joy might we be cheating ourselves out of?

Ironically, it turns out that fear is what prevents us from growing and changing. Fear wants nothing to change; fear demands the status quo. And the status quo leads to death.[3]

Who wants to be status quo? You see, status quo is stagnant and stymied living. On the other hand, compassionate activity is vibrant and fulfilled living.

But we have to muster up quite a bit of courage in order to overcome our fears. For me, it takes work! I admit, reaching out to perfect strangers is frightening. I have to literally force myself to act and place myself around people who do this much more naturally. One such person who has helped me to overcome my fears is a fellow pastor named Keith Marvel.

Keith is one of those natural-born evangelists. It seems like nothing scares this guy! One summer Keith had a great idea about reaching out to

> Most of His opportunities to care and heal occurred because He was out walking among them.

an entire apartment complex in a low-income neighborhood.

He wanted me, as the youth pastor, to help lead it and involve the youth group. I agreed, but I was shaking in my shorts. When we decided to go door-to-door to invite people, I told Keith I would do it, but only if he came with me. (There's a good reason why Jesus sent out his disciples in twos! A lot of them were probably as big a chicken as I am!)

As Keith and I began to go around the complex and tell people about the BBQ and outreach we were having, doors of ministry began to open up right in front of us! People were asking us to pray for them about their drug addictions, and for their children who were sick. Single moms wept as we prayed because Jesus was making Himself so real to them through our prayers. They begged us to come back. And all we did was make the effort to go out and be open to the needs of those we met.

I'm reminded of a parable where Jesus asks us to: "Go out to the highways and hedges, and compel them to come in, that my house may be filled" (Luke 14:23).

So many times we (and I'm the guiltiest of this) sit on our hands and wait for someone who needs help to come knocking on our door. That's the opposite of what we should be doing! Think of how many encounters Jesus had with the sick and with people who were possessed by evil. Most of His opportunities to care and heal occurred because He was out walking among them.

Let's follow His example and put ourselves where the needs are!

The results of that outreach weekend are still vivid in my mind. As the youth band played in the middle of the complex, dozens of people sat at the tables and enjoyed food with the people of our church. The lives of those strangers were affected by love because we took the time to be with them in their world.

And we changed and gained a new perspective on giving of ourselves as we took the friendship of Christ out of the four walls of our church and brought it to those who were hungry for it.

When we parted that day, those people knew what God's love felt like. And we knew reaching out was worth it because of the smiles on our new friends' faces!

Overcoming Our Fear

What is it that fear may be robbing from you? What kind of adventures in the kingdom of God could you be experiencing right now?

It could be that you think you don't have the money—or maybe it's time you don't have to spare? It doesn't matter what the reason is, it's still fear that keeps you from being who God wants you to be. The most important question you have to ask yourself is : *Am I fulfilling the life I know I am called to live? Am I living my destiny?*

The only person who keeps you from finding that kind of life is you. But you can change. We stop being dormant by taking the first step—by coming out of our safe place.

We overcome our fear when we refuse to give the enemy a foothold, and refuse to respond to the fear.

Fear didn't get in the way of Jesus living the kind of life He came to live. He made a life out of helping those who were most needy. He still responds with love to the ones society has turned their backs

> Am I fulfilling the life I know I am called to live? Am I living my destiny?

on. Jesus knew that people—even the dirtiest and most unattractive—are *the* most important in life.

Jesus: Compassion in Action

A story from Luke 7 is a great picture of how Jesus treated people others looked down on—even when He risked being

publicly humiliated and condemned. Jesus had been invited
to have dinner at the house of a Pharisee named Simon.
Remember, a Pharisee was a religious leader of that culture.
They were the ones who knew the Law and fulfilled it. At
least, that's what they claimed.

As Jesus was dining with the "religious elite," a woman
whom the Bible says was a sinner, suddenly crashed the
party and did something that was very socially unacceptable.

This woman approached Jesus and was unexpectedly
overcome with emotion. She wept over His feet. When she
realized Jesus' feet were covered with tears and those tears
were mingled with the dust from the roads, she immediately
began to dry them with her own hair! As if that wasn't enough,

As she stood
before Him, she lost
control of herself and
the tears fell.

she began to kiss His feet. To top it all
off, she broke open a very expensive jar
of perfume she had been saving for her
marriage day (probably worth a year's
wages) and poured it all over His feet.

We can understand a little about where this woman
came from because it seems everyone in town knew she was
a "sinner." At best, that meant she had loose morals. At worst,
she was the town prostitute.

Somewhere in the recent past she must have had an encounter with Jesus. Perhaps it was on the side of the road as He as walked through town, or maybe it was a more private encounter when He took time to speak with her about the pain of personal issues. Whenever it was, she experienced love and forgiveness that went down deep and healed her. Her grateful response manifested itself during this Pharisee's dinner.

I imagine that she merely wanted to thank Jesus for what He had done. Then the gravity of it must have hit her—being overcome by the fact that Jesus knew her sinful past and wicked way of life, and forgave her anyway. She wasn't "that sinner-woman" anymore. She was forgiven and beloved of God. As she stood before Him, she lost control of herself and the tears fell.

But when Simon the Pharisee—the one whose very religious vocation it was to be kind and compassionate—saw what she was doing, he made a statement that exposed his own sinfulness: "If this man were a prophet He would know who and what sort of person this woman is who is touching Him, that she is a sinner" (v. 39 NASB). In other words, if Jesus were the real deal, He would see through this woman, know she lived a sinful life, and send her away like the dog she was!

Because of Simon's zeal to live a perfectly religious life, letting nothing unclean touch him, he missed out on so much!

The sad part is that often you and I play the role of Simon. We hide behind our supposed goodness, when we're really afraid. Simon was scared to enter that lady's world. He feared their differences and what everyone might think. He did what too many of us do in the face of another's deep emotional response. Judge. Run. Ignore the problem. Pretend it isn't there.

Jesus could have been concerned about what everyone might say about this woman crying on His feet. He

> Do something daring to experience the joy and blessing of loving the poor.

could have worried about what rumors could fly. He could have sent her away because her actions embarrassed Him. But instead He embraced her and valued as much as anyone else at the gathering.

And He uses us to show this same love to others—an unconditional love. It's the kind of love that doesn't fear what others think, doesn't fear the nationality, the kind of clothes, car or house, but only sees the heart of a brother or sister and accepts them right where they are.

So in summary, we can overcome our fear by making others' pain a priority in our lives. Remembering, people are eternal, fear is not.

Second, we move to change our lifestyle and start to give sacrificially to the fatherless. This can include our time, energy, and our physical resources.

Finally, we do something daring to experience the joy and blessing of loving the poor.

Bring an outcast woman to the feet of Jesus and let her experience all that causes her to be so grateful all she can do is weep.

Notes from the Field

I'm 40 years old. I never knew my real father. Can you believe at my age, I'm still suffering the pain of that loss? Who would have ever known? I wonder how many men there are out there like me?

Allow me to say a word of thanks. Your acts of kindness, have helped me to see what a true Godly man looks like. Being my friend, inviting me to dinner, asking me to go fishing: these simple acts have helped heal my broken heart. Now, I have the courage to follow your example to my own children.

Your friend,
Steve

Chapter Six

We Are All Cosmic Orphans

erhaps as we've talked about the fatherless, you've sensed an echo of your own life. Sometimes we discover in the stories of the hurting, we find many of our own. Their struggles are our struggles.

At one time or another, many of us have felt the way the fatherless feel. We may have had parents growing up, but the pain we experienced from the ones we called Mom or Dad was just as traumatic as not having parents at all.

Certainly we've all been in places where nobody knows us and we feel like a stranger. Do you remember how it feels to be visiting or living someplace where you are isolated from all familiar faces? And what about the time when tragedy struck and took the life of someone close to you—do you remember the pain and sense of hopelessness?

That's why our heart goes out to the fatherless every time we hear about the pain they deal with. If we're honest with ourselves, it's our pain too and we can empathize. The loss, rejection, hopelessness, and loneliness are emotions we relate to.

The world we live in is full of questions. We all try to make some

> Their struggles have also been our struggles.

sense of them in order to understand the meaning of our existence. We struggle with existential issues such as: Who am I? Why am I so lonely? Why am I having such a difficult time relating to others? Why do I feel hurt and abandoned by those who used to be my friends?[1]

Though the exact issues may be different for each of us, the root of the struggle is not. The truth is, at some point we've all felt the feelings of being fatherless.

Why Reach Out?

It's obvious that one of the reasons God calls His people to reach out to the defenseless is because they are the neediest. Without our help, they die early deaths, they are swept into lives of poverty, they make bad decisions and end up in jail. The people of God can step in and love the fatherless and help them not end up as statistics—we can show them they have a chance to make it in life. You can be a turning point for them by making an effort to express the Father's love in simple ways that make eternal differences.

But another reason for reaching out to the needy may not be as obvious. Inside each of us, a search is taking place. We are looking for what makes us whole.

Do you notice that most of us are never satisfied when we accomplish the next goal? The one thing we think will bring contentment or happiness, fails to really fulfill once it's attained. Maybe it's only the idea of achieving something that makes it so attractive.

That reality should say something to you and me. Possessing things of this earth is merely an empty attempt to satisfy surface needs. But we have needs that run much deeper.

Cosmic Orphans

No matter what we have received in this life, this fact remains: we are all cosmic orphans. We are looking for reasons to explain who we are and where we come from.

Have you ever known someone who was adopted? Often this is the scenario: No matter how loving his adopted parents are, their love just isn't enough to answer the deeper questions. The past is a mystery. His real father and mother are unknown

—he doesn't know what kind of people he comes from. He doesn't feel complete because a major piece of his life is missing that might help him explain his future.

I know what this feels like because I was adopted. I didn't know my real father for the first sixteen years of my life. I used to wonder, *Who is he? Am I anything like him? Does he feel the same things I do? Do I have habits that are like his? Would understanding more about him help to explain any of the problems I have in my life? Where can I find answers that will help me?*

We all need to have these questions answered, but the real need is to have them answered in the spiritual sense. The orphan, widow, stranger, and you and I are all asking the same question: *Who is my true Father?*

This same question must have been at the source of the disciples' panic when Jesus was about to be taken away to be crucified. They were a group of rough and tough, full-grown men who were frightened because Jesus was talking about leaving this earth, about having to die.

Why the fear? Because they had built a relationship with this astonishing person—somebody who had revealed to them the loving heart of God. He had given them perspective and answered some of their deepest questions about who they were, where they came from, and where they were going. Like adopted children who have searched for a parent, they had found their true Father through Jesus.

But He said he was leaving. *How could this be? What would they do? Who would be the brother, teacher, and friend they'd come to depend on? Who would be there to show them the Father's heart?*

When the disciple Simon Peter asked Jesus where He was going, Jesus answered, "Where I go, you cannot follow Me now; but you shall follow later."

Peter's reaction probably spoke of the desperation that was filling all of their minds. Peter cried out, "Lord, why can I not follow You right now?" (John 13:36 NASB).

> The orphan, widow, stranger, and you and I are all asking the same question: Who is my true Father? ◄

Understanding how the disciples must be feeling, Jesus said:

> *Let not your heart be troubled; believe in God, believe also in Me. In My Father's house are many dwelling places; if it were not so, I would have told you; for I go to prepare a place for you. And if I go and prepare a place for you, I will come again, and receive you to Myself; that where I am, there you may be also.* (JOHN 14:1–3)

Jesus encouraged and comforted them, letting them know He was not abandoning them. He was going to take care of things for their future, and He was coming back.

And then Jesus spoke right to the very heart of the matter.

"I will not leave you as orphans; I will come to you."

(JOHN 14:18 NASB)

Why did He use the word *orphan?* Because that's exactly how they felt—and that was exactly what they were—until Jesus came on the scene and revealed God's love.

Through Jesus' love for them, these men had begun to understand and know their true Father. He showed them

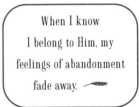

When I know I belong to Him, my feelings of abandonment fade away.

what life was about and how to live it. They were no longer orphans. They were the children of God!

This is the greatest need to be met in our day—to know our true Father. Knowing Him brings definition, fulfillment, and completion to our lives. It truly answers the questions of our existence, yesterday, today, and tomorrow. God is our Father.

Paul assures us of this same truth in the book of Romans.

*You have received a spirit of adoption as sons by
which we cry out, 'Abba! Father!'"*

(ROMANS 8:15 NASB)

That word *Abba* literally means "Daddy." But why do we
need to cry out, "Daddy"? I used to wonder why we use that
term to refer to God.

Now I see. Whether I like to admit it or not, it's because
the greatest cry of my heart is to know my true "Daddy."
When I know I belong to Him, my feelings of abandonment
fade away. I know I am loved unconditionally. I have a purpose
for living and the One who desires to be with me more than
any other will parent me as a perfect Father should.

As the next verse says,

*"The Spirit Himself testifies with our spirit that we
are children of God, and if children, heirs also, heirs of
God and fellow heirs with Christ..."*

(ROMANS 8:16-17 NIV)

We inherit what Christ inherits. We are full-fledged,
card-carrying children of the Father!

We are all beloved children created in the image of God. Our greatest desire is to be singled-out, cherished, and loved in a way that makes us feel like we are significant. Nothing could give us more confidence in this truth than hearing the voice of God saying to us:

> "I have called you by name, from the very begining you are mine and I am yours. You are my beloved. On you my favor rests. I have molded you in the depths of the earth and knitted you together in your mother's womb. I have carved you in the palm of my hand and hidden you in the shadow of my embrace. I look at you with infinite tenderness and care for you with a care more intimate than that of a mother for her child. I have counted every hair on your head and guided you at every step. Wherever you go I go with you, and wherever you rest I keep watch. I will give you food that will satisfy all your hunger and drink that will quench all your thirst. I will not hide my face from you. You know me as your own as I know you as my own. You belong to me...[2]

Where has this journey lead us? To a vast treasure chest with countless gifts to offer. Rememer the places you have traveled and people you have met in these pages.

As you continue down this road of ministering to the fatherless, realize there is still a wealth of treasure to be discovered. This is just a beginning. The more we become the hands, the feet, the love of Jesus, the more joy we find. We give, and we end up receiving much more than we could ever imagine.

After all is said and done, when we sincerely ask God the question, "If I could live my life doing only one thing, what would You want me to do?", I believe the message of Isaiah 58: 7-9 would be His answer:

Is it not to share your food with the hungry,
And to provide the poor wanderer with shelter;
When you see the naked, to clothe him,
And not to turn away from your own flesh and blood?
Then your light shall break forth like the dawn,
and your healing will quickly appear
then your righteousness will go before you;

*and the glory of the L*ORD *will be your rear guard.*

*Then you will call, and the L*ORD *will answer;*

You will cry for help, and He will say: 'Here am I.'

And He *is* here

   . . . with you.

As you walk through the fields of the fatherless.

   Your light will break forth like the morning!

   And the life you live will no longer seem mundane and

meaningless. Instead, every minute will be filled with joy,

purpose, and significance.

   And when this life is over and you stand face-to-face

with the Father, what a reward will be in store for you!

Because you saw the face of Jesus in the face of the lost and lonely,

   God will see His Son in your eyes.

Because you cared about most what He cares most about—

   God will recognize you as His faithful partner.

And because you made every effort

   to express in simple ways the Father's love

      the smallest deeds you did for the least of these

   will count greatly for all eternity.

Thanks for joining me on this journey through
the fields of the fatherless. If you have any thoughts or words
you would like to share, or if you would like me to speak at
your church, group, or organization please contact me at:

tom@fieldsofthefatherless.com
719.487.7800

I'll look for you in the fields of the fatherless!

~ Notes ~

INTRODUCTION

1. Edna Ullmann-Margalit, Social Research, Winter 1988.

CHAPTER 1

1. F. W. Boeham, *The Heavenly Octave* (Grand Rapids: Baker Book House, 1936), 18.

2. Samuel Vinay and Chris Sugden, ed., *Mission as Transformation: A Theology of the Whole Gospel* (Oxford: Regnum Books International, 1999), 411.

3. Sheryl Henderson Blunt, "Bono Tells Christians, Don't Neglect Africa," *Christianity Today*, 22 April 2002, 18.

CHAPTER 3

1. Malcolm Muggeridge, *Something Beautiful for God* (New York: Harper & Row Publishers, 1971), 22.

CHAPTER 4

1. Press Release cb98-228.html, U.S. Census Bureau, www.census.gov, 29 April 1999.

2. "American Agenda," World News Tonight with Peter Jennings, 12 January 1995.

3. Open Doors Statistical Survey, 13 November 2001, www.opendoorsweb.org/Press/International_Students_in_the_US.htm

4. Ken Gire, *The Weathering Grace of God* (Ann Arbor, Michigan: Servant Publications, 2001).

5. The National Summit, Atlanta, Georgia, November 2000 – The CoMission for Children at Risk.

CHAPTER 5

1. Henri Nouwen, *Compassion: A Reflection on the Christian Life* (New York: Image Books, 1983), 4.

2. Ibid.

3. Jean Vanier, *Becoming Human* (New Jersey: Paulist Press, 1998), 73.

CHAPTER 6

1. I am infinitely grateful to Ravi Zacharias for these ideas. For further study on the struggle to finding meaning and understanding these existential issues, please consult Ravi's book, *Can Man Live Without God* (Nashville, Tennessee: Word Publishing, 1997).

2. Henri Nouwen, *Life of the Beloved* (New York: Crossroads Publishing, 1992), 30-31.